The
Praise and Worship

Living Victoriously in the Presence of God

Gabriel Rogers

*The Power of Praise and Worship Living Victoriously in
The Presence of God*

Scripture quotations are taken from the *King James Version*
of the Bible.

Additional Scripture quotations taken from *Praise and
Worship Study Bible* copyright © 1997 by The Livingstone
Corporation. All rights reserved.

Additional Scripture quotations taken from *New King James
Version* copyright © 1982 by Thomas Nelson, Inc. All rights
reserved.

Additional Scripture quotations taken from *Who Was Who in
the Bible: the Ultimate A to Z Resource* copyright © 1999
by Thomas Nelson, Inc. All rights reserved.

For emphasis, the author has placed Bible quotations in
italics.

For emphasis, the author has placed some Bible quotations
in italics and bold print.

ISBN 1-931600-13-9

This book is respectfully dedicated to my parents
William and Lillie Rogers; you two are the reason
why I'm here, thank you. Also in memory of my
deceased Pastor, Dr. Lorenzo L. Woods
"he started it all."

Acknowledgments

First and foremost I would like to thank my Lord, my Savior, and my Source Jesus Christ. Without Christ, I realize that I am nothing. I would also like to thank my spiritual father, Bishop Kevin Long; the impact you have made on my life will never be forgotten. To my spiritual mother Dr. Wanda Turner; I appreciate your love and mentoring, you are one of God's greatest leaders. To Bishop Turner; every time I talk to you my vision expands. To my biological father and mother, William and Lillie; I love you both and thank you for bringing me up in the fear of the Lord. To my brothers and sister Greg Rogers, Minister Geary Rogers, Pastor Glenn Rogers and Melanie Rogers; you all are a real life depiction of awesome, I love you all and thank you for being a great support system. To my whole family; you all mean so much to me, thanks. To my best friend, Pastor Anthony Freeman, I appreciate you. To my church family; Temple, you all are a model of what worship looks like, "keep your fire." To my administrator Deborah and all of my readers Gogi, Kris and Lillie you all are irreplaceable, thanks. To all of the people who were obstacles in my life, this book would not have been possible without you, thank you. Finally to everyone else who has impacted my life in a positive way, I love you and thank you so much for being instruments of God.

Contents

Introduction

Beloved, we are living in a time in which it is essential for us to maximize God's holy presence. As believers we must learn how to move from just experiencing God's presence, to actually living *in* his presence. Contrary to popular belief, our heavenly father has not called us to be the devil's prey or to live defeated lives. There is one place in the spiritual realm in which you can experience a sense of "total peace". The fact of the matter is that praise and worship encompasses much more than our traditional rituals. Saints of God, you need to know that praise and worship actually gives us the power to live.

In order for the body of Christ to excel to new dimensions, it is essential that we understand the power of praise and worship. Praise and worship gives us, the believers, access to the very presence of God. We as the body of Christ must realize that through praise and worship we have the power to destroy every yoke (form of bondage) in our lives and obtain everything we need. I propose to you that if we, as the body of Christ, actually knew the power of getting into the presence of God, we would literally revolutionize our daily living experiences. Our heavenly father has empowered us to live life in the overflow. The main characteristic of the overflow is living constantly in the concentrated presence of God. As you read this book, I challenge you to apply all of the messages to your personal life.

It is essential that we not limit praise and worship to a "Sunday morning experience". We must have a broader scope on living in the power of praise and worship. Praise and worship has so many advantages. When praise and worship is operating in your life, you experience the profound manifestations of God's presence. The fact of the matter is this, Sunday morning praise" alone, will not birth you into the promises God has for you. It's going to take a lifestyle of praise and worship. *"2 Timothy 3:5 Having a form of Godliness, but denying the power thereof: from such turn away."*

We as believers today can gather a powerful revelation from Paul's (above) instructions to Timothy. I believe that as Paul was instructing on the perilous times, he implies that it is simply hypocritical to have some of God. We as worshipers not only should have a form of God (our ceremonial praise and shout), but we need to literally have the power of God evident in our life. As believers we have to realize that everything we need from God is contained in our praise and worship. In this book, we will point out specific individuals that lead victorious lives through the power of praise and worship. Throughout this book, I hope to prove to you that, the power (anointing) of praise and worship will bring deliverance, healing, money and everything else that is a part of living in the "Zoë", which is the God kind of life. Many people live defeated lives because they are yet to tap into the power of praise and worship. Real praise and worship will give birth to every vision and purpose in your life. I challenge you to get ready for major transitions in your life, as you understand the power of praise and worship.

What is Praise?

The Life Application Bible describes praise as: *"A means to commend or give honor."* When we commend somebody we commend him or her because of something he or she has done. For the sake of this discussion, praise is simply the act of giving thanks for a specific purpose. Praise is both proactive and reactive. Praise is proactive in that it is done in advance. Before there is major breakthrough of any kind, there must be major praise! When you praise God in advance, you exercise what I believe, is the highest form of faith.

Hebrews 11:1 "Now faith is the substance of things hoped for, the evidence of things not seen."

When you praise God in advance you act as if you already have the thing that you are praising God for. In the onset, we have to grasp the concept that a proactive praise is futuristic for us but present for God. In other words we operate in what's to come but God operates on our behalf in the now. The Lord has a funny kind of way of making our future wishes a present reality when we praise him in advance. Metaphorically speaking, if my father promises me a brand new car, I don't wait to thank him for the car when I get the manifestation of the car. Because I trust my daddy and his word, I began to thank him right now for the new car. In other words, you don't need the tangible manifestation of the blessing to praise God; you praise God because of the promise of the manifestation. The Lord wants us to be in a place in which we began to thank him in the "now" for what he has already promised us. That is why the word of God says in Hebrews 11:1 *"Now Faith is the substance of things hoped for, the evidence of things not seen."* You have to understand that along with "now" faith you need a "now" praise." Faith is the understanding that God is going to do just what he said he would do. Praising, based on faith, is the equivalent to praising God on credit. Let me tell you this one thing, God has the very best credit! If God has truly spoken something, you can bet that it is going to come to past. Thus saints of God, my definition of faith is, **"PRAISE GOD LIKE YOU ALREADY GOT IT."**

Praise is reactive in that it acknowledges those things that the Lord has brought forth in our lives. The worst kind of child is one who does not appreciate those things that his/her parent does on the child's behalf. Take a moment now and visualize your family structure. If you are a parent you are more apt to give to the child that has proven to be thankful in times past. In other words, a simple "thank you" from your child can change the course of his/her future in receiving gifts. Our heavenly father is very similar to us in his methods of giving. The Lord remembers who said thank you for their last break through. Not praising God after he gives you a blessing is like burning a bridged that you have crossed. What you must understand is that we all have a spiritual bank account with God. The withdrawals we

11

make are the blessings we pray for and receive. When we make a withdrawal from this spiritual account, there must be a deposit of praise. By praising God, you enlarge your spiritual bank account. One of the worst things you can do is get a major blessing from the Lord and forget to say thank you. What then is the purest form of thank you? A real and sincere praise is the purest form of thank you. In a nutshell, my present act of thanks sets me up for future blessings. If you want God to bless you, you must learn how to bless him! David, one of the most popular icons in the Christian faith, knew how to bless the Lord.

Psalm 34:1 "I will bless the Lord at all times and his praise shall continually be in my mouth."

I chose David because while he had many faults, he always had a sense of Godly fear for the presence of God. If you read the story of David, you'll find that he had many shortcomings, but one thing David understood was the importance of praise. I am not at all saying that we should live a life of sin. What I am saying is that your attitude of praise positions you for the heart of God. Let me explain my theory. In spite of all of David's flaws, both 1 Samuel 13:14 and Acts 13:22 affirm David as a man after God's own heart. Because David was after God's own heart, every other king of Judah after David was compared to him and the model he established for reigning. Not only did David's reputation of greatness go throughout the Old Testament but it also carried over into the New Testament as he is described in the book of Acts. I submit to you that in order to be after God's own heart, you must be one who has a sincere praise. David obviously did not live perfectly because he committed adultery with Bath-Sheba, just to mention one of his flaws. There were two major things David knew how to do, he knew how to ask for forgiveness and he knew how to praise God with all of his might. What then qualifies me to be after God's own heart? Number one, I am chosen by God and secondly, I must be willing ready and able to, like David, "bless the Lord at all times." Understand this major point, by the mere fact that you are saved, you can rest assure that God has chosen you. As you seek destiny and purpose, you must accompany your search with praise.

The writer of the 150 Psalm gives us a solid explanation of praise and how it is done. *"Praise ye the Lord. Praise God in his sanctuary: praise him in the firmament of his power. 2 Praise him for his mighty acts: praise him according to his excellent greatness. 3 Praise him with the sound of the trumpet: Praise him with the psaltery and harp. 4 praise him with the timbrel and dance: Praise him with the stringed instruments and organs. 5 Praise him upon the loud cymbals: praise him upon the high sounding cymbals. 6 Let everything that hath breath praise ye the Lord. Praise the Lord."*

The writer of this Psalm, who is anonymous, had his ear to the heart of God concerning praise. He lets us know in verse 2 of the 150th Psalm that praise is done in response to those things that God does for us. In other words, we praise him for his mighty acts. It is our responsibility to be aware of God's mighty acts concerning our lives.

Understand that a mighty act is major deliverance in our lives, but it's also God's ability to keep our hearts beating all day and night (now if you ask me, that's a mighty act!). With that being said, we must constantly be aware of the fact that no matter what is going on, praise is always in order. I would like to interject a slight curve here. We give God praise in response to the positive blessings He releases into our lives, but we should also praise him in response to our adversity. When we praise him in response to problems and hardship, we let the kingdom of hell know that our praise is deeper than just an emotional fix. *It is important to be ready to lift up a praise when all hell has broken loose in your life!* If the truth were told, we don't have an earthly solution for many of the problems we face in our everyday living. Since we can't figure out many of our problems, why don't we just let God work it out! Praise is a faith vehicle that says, *God I trust you and I know that while I am praising, you are working on my behalf.* The strength of our afflictions can sometimes be directly related to our spiritual warfare or the lack thereof. When you refuse to praise God in the midst of adversity, you accept the fate of the enemy. God has a plan for your life but so does Satan. Your praise keeps Satan in check. Let me help you understand what I am saying. "It is not adversity that defines us, it is the *response* to adversity that defines us." In other words, the devil is not going to stop attacking you, but your attitude and action of praise will constantly put the enemy to flight. In understanding praise, it is important to note the purpose of praise.

Praise is your spiritual weapon against the enemy. Allow me to pause for a moment in order to explain the vitality of praise.

Ephesians 6:10 "For we wrestle not against flesh and blood, but against principalities, against powers, against the rulers of the darkness of this world, against spiritual wickedness in high places."

In the above verse, Paul gives us insight on the forces we are battling against. You cannot fight a spirit without understanding the spiritual realm.

I would like to interject a very important point here. Saint of God, there is a constant war going on in the spiritual realm. There are angels who are battling on our behalf when we praise.

Psalm 34:7 "For the angel of the LORD guards all who fear him, and he rescues them."

Your spiritual weapon of praise literally summons the warring angels. God's angels bring your blessings and deliverance.

Daniel 9:21-22 "I was praying, Gabriel, whom I had seen in the earlier vision, came swiftly to me at the time of the evening sacrifice. 22 He explained to me, "Daniel, I have come here to give you insight and understanding."

Now notice in the above verses that the Angel Gabriel comes to Daniel with vital information. The information Daniels receives is from God but brought by an angel. The vision Daniel receives from Gabriel is symbolic of him knowing the next phase of his life. Knowing the next phase of your life is called vision. One of the biggest blessings you can receive is vision. In other words, Gabriel is assigned to deliver vision, Daniel's blessing.

Daniel 10:12 "Then he said, "Don't be afraid, Daniel, Since the first day you began to pray for understanding and to humble yourself before your God, your request has been heard in heaven. I have come to answer your prayer."

Notice in the above verse that Daniel has been in a humbled state and in much prayer. In other words, Daniel was in supplication, which is a higher form of prayer mixed with worship. The delivering angel comes to bring the blessing but the angel gives an explanation for why he was late.

Daniel 10:13 "But for twenty-one days the spirit prince if the kingdom of Persia blocked my way. Then Michael, one of the archangels, came to help me, and I left him there with the spirit prince of the kingdom of Persia."

The above scripture points out that a demonic spirit was holding up the angel with the blessing. Daniel had to wait an extra three weeks for his blessing to get through. It wasn't until Michael, a warring angel, came and occupied the demon so that the angel delivering the blessing was able to go free. My stance is this, when you praise God, you summon and strengthen the angelic army so that your blessings can be released. Before Daniel received the blessing of knowing what was next for him and his people, there was a war in the spirit. Understand that there are some visions and blessings that can't be released until you do proper warfare in the spirit. I'd like to pose a question. If Daniel's blessing was held up for three weeks, how long will your blessings be held up?" I submit to you this thought, the more praise the quicker the release of your blessing. The angel carrying your blessing is moving at a pace that reflects your praise. Understand saint of God that some angels are only designed to carry the blessing. The Angel Gabriel was not equipped to fight off the spirit of Persia. My point is this; the thing you have been praying for has been released from heaven for a long time now. What you need to know is that God heard you the very first time you prayed and he answered you. The angel delivering your blessing is not equipped to fight, you have to summon the warring angel through your praise or your blessing will be continually held up.

Saints of God, you cannot fight spirits with your earthly insights. Many people feel that they can battle the host of hell with their education, money or other economical means. When disease is trying to attack your body and the doctor does not have the answer, your money and education is powerless. *The fact of the matter is that the only form of opposition that demons understand is solid and sincere praise!* The devil's goal is to steal your praise. Jesus tells us in John 10:10, Satan comes to steal, kill and destroy. Beloved let me explain something very important to you. The enemy does not need or want your car, money, house or any material thing attached to you. I know that this goes against the traditional view of the enemy, but what Satan wants is your soul. He wants your emotions your will and your intellect.

He will seek to get your soul by attacking everything around you but ultimately he wants your soul. In order to get your soul he must get rid of your praise. If the devil can get you to shut up and sit down in the midst of trouble, his mission is accomplished. If Satan can take your praise, he can ultimately kill you. Satan wants to destroy your vision. Your vision is larger than just your accomplishments; your vision encompasses generations to come. If the enemy steals your praise, he will destroy the hope of your future generations. I hope you understand how important praise is. Praise will give birth to your promise, therefore, the lack of praise causes your promise to be aborted. When you stand up and praise anyhow, you cross over into a place of faith in which God can really step in on your behalf.

In verses 3 thru 5 of the 150th Psalm, the writer explains how praise is done. In reviewing these three verses it is quite evident that praise for the most part, is loud and expressive. The writer names at least seven major instruments along with the art of dance to help us to understand the act of praise. It is obvious that praise is very expressive and is used to show an individual how much he or she is appreciated. I believe that the writer named so many instruments to illustrate the fact that God is worthy of so much. As a matter of fact, the writer of the 150th Psalm mentioned cymbals twice, which gives me the exciting revelation that God is worthy of double the praise we offer to him. You can never praise God enough. It is interesting how in the Old Testament, many of the people praised on their way to the battle, during the battle and after the victory. It is obvious then that God is worthy to be praised at all times.

In our synopsis of praise, we have specific instructions on who is allowed to praise. It is important that we realize that everyone on earth has the right and command to praise the Lord. In 6th verse of Psalm 150, the writer says; "let everything that hath breath praise the Lord". Praise invites the believer as well as the unbeliever. No matter the lifestyle, everyone has a right to praise the Lord. As we watch secular artists on television receive awards, in many cases they always give honor or praise to the Lord. Now the fruit of the artists prove that they are not a believer, but they still have the right to acknowledge Jesus for their gift, (*"For the gifts and calling of God are without repentance" Romans 11:29*). Please understand that those who do not repent will not live eternally with God. I do not want to give you the misconception that praise is a ticket to heaven because it's not. Let me inform you of this very important fact. "You can praise your way straight to hell." I want to make this disclosure because in many places we have transformed the church into a house of prostitution. In other words, we want the goods God has to offer without the cross that comes with knowing him. Child of God, you can dance, sing and shout without relationship with God and totally "miss heaven." The last verse of the 150th Psalm simply states, *"Praise the Lord"*. The writer gives us a command. Not only do we have a right to praise the Lord, we are literally sanctioned by God himself to give him the praise. When you give God the praise, you position yourself for an encounter with Jesus. Praise destroys every distraction in the spiritual atmosphere. If you really want to frustrate the enemy, learn how to praise God in every situation and environment.

What is Worship?

While praise is all-inclusive, worship is left to the believer. Worship is an act that is offered from one's spirit. Worship is internal first and is then expressed externally. Real worship will cause you to flow out of your character. Understand that I am not advocating disorderly worship; what I am saying is that true worship occurs in situations where pride doesn't exist. Allow me to explain on another level. When you are really engulfed in worship, you could care less about the tailored made suit you are wearing, your new hairstyle or any other forms of beautification. When you are really in worship, "time is no longer of the essence." True worship causes you to ignore any distractions and focus totally on getting in the presence of God. When we are in real worship we do not have any ulterior motives (we are not looking for a new car, more money, a spouse or anything else), in true worship you just want to get close to Jesus. The paradox of worship is this; while worship should be done without ulterior motives, you don't have any choice but to be blessed when you worship God.

John 4:23-24 "But the hour cometh, and now is, when the true worshippers shall worship the father in spirit and in truth: for the father seeketh such to worship him. 24 God is a Spirit: and they that worship him must worship him in spirit and in truth."

In the above scripture Jesus himself gives us instructions on worship and who has access to worship. As Jesus addressed the Samaritan woman in John chapter four, he first rebukes her because she lies about her marital status. In his rebuke, Jesus causes a deep spirit of humility to come over the woman, (which is symbolic of the attitude we should have when we are worshiping). When the woman is rebuked she becomes true to herself and Jesus, thus she is transformed into a worshipper. Understand that the woman's flaws are exposed to Jesus and she has nothing to hide. God wants us to be honest in our worship. When we are honest we are validated as true worshippers. As worshippers, we often use postures of bowing, lifting hands, and laying prostrate. All of the major postures of worship put us in humbled or surrendering positions. As humbled worshippers, we let God know that we are literally nothing with out his presence. We like the woman at the well are transformed into true worshippers. In the fourth chapter of John, Jesus lets us know what he is looking for in terms of a worshipper. The specific instruction is that our heavenly father is looking for someone to worship him in spirit and in truth.

It is common knowledge that Satan, our adversary, does not have the spirit of truth because he works on the basis of deception.

John 8:44 "Ye are of your father the devil and the lusts of your father ye will do. He was a murderer from the beginning, and **abode not in truth**, *because* **there is no truth in him**. *When he speaketh a lie, he speaketh of his own: for* **he is a liar, and the father of it."**

One must then ask the question, how can an individual who has not received Christ worship in truth? The answer is simple. That individual cannot worship Christ in truth, because he still belongs to Satan. The individual who flows under deception has an incomplete relationship with Jesus. In John the 8th chapter, Jesus clearly acknowledges that those who are not believers are the children of Satan. I must point out that children automatically take the spirit of their father. A father who is a liar transfers a lying spirit to his children. Worship is an act of truth. When we worship we must be admissive of our flaws and recognize that Christ is our redeemer and fulfiller. These factors don't allow us, the believers, to get the big head because worship is an act that calls for constant confession of our inconsistencies. As a worshipper, you develop an acute hunger for God's presence. If you think praise has some benefits, let me tell you what worship does. Worship impregnates you with blessings from the Lord. Worship also delivers the blessing that the Lord has conceived in your womb. For an example, let's look at Hannah who was the mother of Samuel.

*1 Samuel 5-6 "But Hannah he gave a worthy portion; for he loved Hannah: but the **Lord had shut up her womb.** 6 And her adversary also provoked her sore, for to make her fret, because the **Lord had shut up her womb.**"*

First things being first, let's point out that the Lord had shut Hannah's womb. This goes against the theory that everything that's perceived to be negative comes from Satan. The word says that the Lord had shut up Hannah's womb. Many of the afflictions we suffer are God sent. One thing to keep in mind is that a "God sent affliction" always has purpose behind it. My point is this, since the Lord had Hannah's womb shut up, he obviously wanted to get something from her and to her. While Hannah's womb is shut she goes through much pain and ridicule.

1 Samuel 1:6 "And her adversary also provoked her sore, for to make her fret, because the Lord had shut up her womb."

While you are in your dry season, when it seems like God has gone deaf, you will sometimes feel alienated and isolated. But let's look at what Hannah does in her dry season.

1 Samuel 1:11 "And she vowed a vow, and said, O Lord of hosts, if thou wilt indeed look on the affliction of thine handmaid, but wilt give unto thine handmaid a man child, then I will give him unto the Lord all the days of his life, and there shall no razor come upon his head."

Hannah makes God a promise, that if he would bless her with a child she would dedicate the child back to him. Thus our first point of being ready for conception in worship is an attitude that says, "God whatever you bless me with during my worship, I am willing to give it back to you." Let me explain it another way in the natural. Before a prospective mother can conceive a child, her body temperature has to be right. In other words, before you can conceive the blessing, your spiritual body temperature must be right. Your attitude has to be in a place of total submission to the Spirit of God. Understand that Hannah is distraught and in a place of expectancy at the same time.

1 Samuel 14-15 "And Eli said unto her, How long wilt thou be drunken? Put away thy wine from thee. 15 And Hannah answered and said, No, my lord, I am a woman of sorrowful spirit: I have drunk neither wine nor strong drink, but I have poured out my soul before the Lord."

Understand now than Hannah, who is totally broken, finally gets to a place where she can make her petition known to Eli. Eli is symbolic of the man of God in this context. Before she got to the man of God, Hannah had poured out her soul before the Lord. I submit this important point. As Hannah poured out her soul before the Lord, Eli was being prepared by God to deliver the pronouncing blessing over Hannah. Let me explain. Worship God even when you don't think he's hearing. While it seems like God is ignoring you, he is really just preparing the pronouncement of the blessing over your life! If you can visualize this, the longer the wait the bigger the pronouncement, now that's exciting! Now listen to what Eli, the man of God, pronounces over Hannah's life.

1 Samuel 1:17 Then Eli answered and said , Go in peace: and the God of Israel grant thee thy petition that thou has asked of him."

As you can see in the above verse, Eli pronounces the blessing. Now look at the faith Hannah exhibits in the next verse.

*1 Samuel 1:18 "And she said, Let thine handmaid find grace in thy sight. So the women went her way, and did eat, and **her countenance was no more sad."***

I put the last phrase in bold print because I really want you to catch this. Once God pronounces the blessing over your life and gives you a glimpse of what you are about to receive, you can dry your eyes! Before God impregnates you in worship, he wants you to believe him at his word. When you believe that what you have been praying is going to be a reality, in the spirit realm you are one day away from conception. Hannah believed God so much so that she stop crying, she stopped worrying and she started eating again. Beloved when God speaks over your life, you can take whatever he says to the bank because it has got to come to past.

*1 Samuel 19-20 "And they rose up in the morning early, and **worshipped before the Lord**, and returned, and came to their house to Ramah: and Elkanah knew Hannah his wife; and the Lord remembered her. 20 Wherefore it came to pass, when the time was come about after Hannah had conceived, that she bare a son, and **called his name Samuel, saying, Because I have asked him of the Lord."***

I put in boldface two very important statements in the above verse. The first statement is **"worshipped before the Lord."** If you are in fact going to give birth, you must worship before, during and after conception. Hannah poured out before her conception, worshipped during conception and if you read the 28th verse of 1st Samuel, chapter one, you will find out that Hannah worshipped after she received the promise of Samuel. Never forget to say thank you after you have received that which was conceived in worship. Because Hannah made good on her promise to dedicate Samuel, she gave birth to three more sons and two daughters. I want you to see this. Hannah, who was barren at one point, not only gets what she prayed for, she gets three more sons and two daughters. Allow me to make a New Testament connection here.

Ephesians 3:20 "Now unto him who is able to do **exceedingly abundantly above all that we ask** *or think, according to the power that worketh in us."*

I am certain that when Hannah prayed and worshipped for Samuel, she had no idea what the Lord really had in store for her. All of the ridicule and pain she went through to have Samuel was worth it because she got a total of six children for the price of one. Hear me child of God, as you worship the almighty God, understand that what he has in store for you is not just what you have been praying for; it's what you've been praying for plus what God wants you to have!

Hannah makes a second statement of major importance in 1 Samuel 1:20. The statement she made was this, *"called his name Samuel because I have asked him of the Lord."* Make sure that the blessing you are asking for is named to give God the glory. Everything conceived in worship must be dedicated to God because the very act of worship is a dedication to God. Saints of God, let me reiterate this important point; Remember to worship the Lord for your conception *in the spirit.* Don't wait until the baby is here, began to sing unto the Lord while that baby is growing inside of you. On your free time, please read 1 Samuel 2:1-10 and Luke 1:46-55. Mary who gave birth to the ever so famous Jesus and Hannah who gave birth to Samuel sang very similar songs after they found out they were going to give birth. When you find out that you're going to give birth, start singing a love song of appreciation, because what God has promised has got to come to past.

A Lifestyle of Praise and Worship

As children of God, it is important for us to realize that when we live a lifestyle of praise and worship, we literally share in God's power. One of our greatest examples of a worshipper in the Old Testament is Moses. Moses led a lifestyle of worship. In order to validate Moses for our discussion, we must first point out his worship.

Exodus 34:8 "And Moses made haste, and bowed his head toward the earth, and worshipped."

Being that Moses was a worshipper, he, had the privilege of being God's friend.

*Exodus 33:11 "And the Lord spake unto Moses face to face, as a man speaketh unto his **friend.**"*

There is absolutely nothing that makes Moses have more rights than we have. The God we serve is no respecter of persons, so why can't we be God's friends also? When one is considered a friend, he/she is allowed privileges that the general population doesn't have. I give to my friends more liberally than I give to anyone. The nature of God is to bless those in whom he knows. We as worshippers have got to realize that when we become God's friend, he is excited about moving on our behalf. I am using Moses because he was hungry for God's presence. When we become Hungry for the presence of God, our heavenly father makes haste on our behalf. One songwriter put it best when he said "Can't nobody do me like Jesus, He's my friend." The thought of having Jesus as a friend excites me in a major way!

Exodus 33:17 "And the Lord said unto Moses, I will do this thing also that thou hast spoken: for thou hast found grace in my sight, and I know thee by name."

The above scripture makes a major disclosure, God knew Moses' name. I believe that this scripture is very symbolic. I want you to think back to when you were in elementary school. During the first week or so of school, the teacher probably used a roster to call out the names of all of the students. By the second or third week of school, the teacher got to know you and your classmates and he/she no longer needed the roster. The teacher knew you because the two of you were together for at least six hours out of the day therefore, she knew you by name. Thus, this illustration brings us to the point that in order for God to know us by name, we must be willing to spend quality time with him. Too much television and leisure activity can easily take away from your time with God, thus crippling your power and purpose. Saints of God, it is crucial for you to understand that the Lord wants to share with you in an up close and intimate way. The more time you spend with God in worship, the more comfortable he will become with you. When God gets comfortable with you, your spiritual ears become more sensitive to the fact that God is talking. While God is always speaking, it's up to us to be in a place to hear what he is saying. You can hear what God is saying by creating an atmosphere for him to elevate his voice. *If you make God feel at home, he will change the whole atmosphere of your house.* Let me explain, if I were to visit your house and you looked at me funny, I probably wouldn't stay long. I mean if I really felt uncomfortable I probably would get up and leave. On the other hand if you made me feel at home, I probably would sit down, relax and share with you. The Holy Spirit has much personality, when he feels at home; he will sit down and share with you in an intimate way. On the other hand, when the Holy Spirit does not feel at home he will allow his glory to depart.

Exodus 24:18 "And Moses went into the midst of the cloud, and gat him up into the mount: and Moses was in the mount forty days and forty nights."

Moses made a conscious decision to leave all of the cares of life and enter into God's presence. We can learn a valuable lesson here. In order to be a worshipper, one has to be willing to spend time with God and sacrifice the cares of this world. Sacrificing the cares of this world does not mean that you are not aware of those things going on around you. Sacrificing the cares of this world simply means that you put God first in the midst of a demanding environment. Time with God must be a priority for you. I even encourage you to, in your daily planner, write in what I call

"GOD TIME". You will be surprised at the amount of peace you experience as a result of your time with God. "**GOD TIME**" will help you to put things into perspective and cause you to understand where you are in your divine destiny. Your destiny and purpose is the only place in life in which you will find total peace.

Sharing In the Power of God

As worshippers, we have the privilege to share in God's power. By sharing in God's power, we literally assume the role of God in our lives. In assuming the role of God, we have the power to change God's mind concerning our environment. I am well aware that my theory of changing God's mind is controversial; hence I have deemed it necessary to provide specific examples:

Exodus 9:10 "Now therefore let me alone, that my wrath may wax hot against them, and that I may consume them: and I will make thee a great nation."

In the above verse, God tells Moses to allow him to devour the Israelites because of their evil ways. The Lord also promises Moses that he will make him a great nation. In other words, the Lord was going to adequately provide for Moses but he was going to destroy the people. So we understand that the Lord's intentions are to cause mass destruction of the Israelites.

Exodus 9:12 "Wherefore should the Egyptians speak, and say, For mischief did he bring them out, to slay them in the mountains, and to consume them from the face of the earth? **Turn from thy fierce wrath, and repent of this evil against thy people."**

Here, Moses instructs God to repent; in other words, Moses tells God to change his mind concerning the people.

Exodus 9:14 "And the Lord **repented** *of the evil which he thought to do unto his people."*

Thus our point is affirmed. We notice that Moses instructs God concerning his judgment to wipe out the people. Moses changes God's mind by reminding him of the promises he made concerning the children of Israel. We must keep in mind that Moses is a worshipper. A worshipper is in the presence of God, therefore, he can both hear and speak to God. I wonder what would have happened if Moses were not in the presence of God. Would the children of Israel have been destroyed? How many of us accept our fate in life because we miss what God is saying concerning our environment and us? There are many things and situations that we have the power to change.

Another example of a worshipper who changed God's mind is Hezekiah.

Isaiah 37:16 "O Lord of host, God of Israel, that dwellest between the cherubims, thou art the God, even thou alone, of all the kingdoms of the earth: thou hast made heaven and earth."

In the text, we see an example of Hezekiah's worship. Since Hezekiah was a worshipper, we can then assume that the mighty acts that the Lord performed on his behalf had something to do with his relationship with God.

41

Isaiah 38:2 "Then Hezekiah turned his face to the wall, and prayed to the Lord."

After Hezekiah had gotten the word of the Lord from the prophet Isaiah that he was going to die, he petitioned God for a change of his word. Now keep in mind that Hezekiah was a worshipper. I must then ask the question, why did Hezekiah deem it necessary to turn to the wall? I mean if Hezekiah was really sick, why didn't he just pray in his current posture? Obviously, Hezekiah was very sick. It must have been painful to move while he was bed stricken. I believe that Hezekiah's turning to the wall was symbolic of his attempt to sacrifice worship to God even in his current adversity. Saints of God, there are going to be times in your life when even turning to the wall will be difficult. What you must grasp is this; *a slight turn in your posture, will cause a major turn in your destiny!* My attempt to turn in lieu of my situation motivates God to move miraculously on my behalf.

Isaiah 38:5 "Go, and say to Hezekiah, Thus saith the Lord, the God of David thy father, I have heard thy prayer, I have seen thy tears: behold, I will add unto thy days fifteen years."

After Hezekiah prays in verse 3, he gets the word that God as extended or added fifteen more years to his life. In other words, the above verse clearly portrays that God changed his mind concerning his original decision for Hezekiah. Now, before we, the worshippers, get the big head with changing God's mind, I must bring clarity. Understand that yes, we do change God's mind, but God who is omniscient (all knowing), already is aware of the fact that he is going to change his mind. In others words, God knows the outcomes of our situations even before they happen. The thing that we must understand is that God knows the outcome but we don't! As worshippers, we must be so close to God to be aware of when to move God's hand concerning our lives. When we are close to God, like Moses and Hezekiah, we can move his power in our direction. When we began to move God's power in our direction, we get a better understanding of the **"Power of Praise and Worship."**

43

The 2 or 3 Principle

In this season that the body of Christ is in, the topic of praise and worship has become prevalent in our church settings. Saints of God, there is so much power in *corporate* praise and worship! There is a simple concept that I have titled "The 2 or 3 Principle."

Matthew 18:18-20 "Verily I say unto you, whatsoever ye shall bind on earth shall be bound in heaven: and whatsoever ye shall loose on earth shall be loosed in heaven."

Now notice that scripture gives us a dialogue on the type of power we have. We literally control heaven's ammunition, but notice "who" the power is given **to**.

*Matthew 18:19 "Again I say unto you, That if **two** of you shall agree on earth as touching any thing that they shall ask, it shall be done for them of my Father which is in heaven."*

The power to bind and loose is given to the "2" which is reflective of an assembly. All you need is one more person who will agree with you in worship and you can control the power of heaven!

*Matthew 18:20 "For where **two or three** are **gathered** together in my name, there am I in the midst of them."*

It is safe to say that the presence of the Lord will reside in places which two or three are found agreeing. In order for the saints to agree, we must be on one accord invoking the presence of God. There is only one way to invoke God's presence; it's called *praise and worship*. Suffice it to say that 1+1 equals a church. Let me clarify that I am not encouraging anyone to start a church or a movement. My simple claim is this; when you combine with another worshipper, you posses the power to loose blessings in your life and bind adversities. The gathering of the children of God is essential to moving the hand of God.

Very recently many of our local churches have made great transitions in terms of our style of what I call *"ceremonial worship."* For the sake of this book, I would like to define *ceremonial worship* as the process of coming together in our church settings and designating a formal allotted time for entering into the concentrated presence of God. In many cases, our churches have or are transitioning from the traditional devotional and testimonial services to now what we call praise and worship. As a praise and worship leader, I am of course, a strong advocate for ceremonial praise and worship.

Hebrews 10:25 "And let us not neglect our meeting together, as some people do, but encourage and warn each other, especially how that the day of his coming back again is drawing near."

The above scripture clearly points out the fact that it is important for us to assemble together as believers. When we assemble together in worship, our spiritual weapons of warfare are joined together creating an arsenal that the enemy cannot contend with. Our Heavenly Father desires to visit our worship services and empower the people of God to break the shackles that are binding them. When the children of God combine their praise and worship, there are corporate blessings and breakthroughs that will take place.

Paul and Silas are examples of **two** men that assembled and performed the miraculous.

*Acts 16:25-26 "And at midnight Paul and Silas prayed, and sing **praises** unto God: and the prisoners heard them. 26 And suddenly there was a great earthquake, so that the foundations of the prison were shaken: and immediately all the doors were opened, and every one's bands were loosed."*

Paul and Silas, **two** servants of the Lord, have been locked up in prison after casting a spirit out of a girl. These **two** men began to pray and sing praises. In others words, Paul and Silas had a worship service. While Paul and Silas are giving God the praise, the jailhouse begins to rock. In our local assemblies, there has got to be praise that will cause God to respond. When God responds, he breaks the shackles in our lives that hold us captive. God will rock your personal jailhouse when you involve yourself in corporate praise. The significance of Paul and Silas's worship is this. When they gave God the praise, not only were they freed, but also all the prisoners around them went free. In other words, those who were in bondage received deliverance because **two** men assembled together in praise. Saints of God, there are many people that are depending on the church to assemble for their deliverance. When the church begins to bless the Lord, everything that is held captive must be liberated. As a result of **two** men worshipping, there was a corporate blessing. In our local church, we must realize that God wants to bless both the church body and the individuals. Not only does the Lord deliver as a result of corporate praise, he also adds to the church.

Acts 16:30-31 "And brought them out, and said, Sirs, what must I do to be saved? 31 And they said, Believe on the Lord Jesus Christ, and thou shalt be saved, and thy house."

The man asking how to be saved was the soldier who held Paul and Silas captive in the prison. Paul and Silas witnessed to the man, in turn getting the man saved and adding on to the church. Notice, the man that was saved was on the outside of the jail cell, symbolizing that he was not apart of those within the four walls. As a result of the praise inside the prison, the outside environment was affected. When you praise God in your local assemblies, your community will change for the better. The Lord wants the body of Christ to move from being a four-walled church to a kingdom, which is translated, *"A church without walls."* I submit to you that the most effective way to grow a church is through sincere praise that both break the chains of the enemy and gives God the glory. It is essential that we plug into the corporate praise and worship power outlets that are available to us. While we are growing the corporate church (our local assemblies), we must also develop the church that lies within each of us individually.

A Sacrifice of Praise

Being a worshipper will sometimes cause you to give up some things that you may hold very close to your heart. We also need to be informed that sometimes we must praise and worship without the feeling. After a long hard day, shouting hallelujah may be the furthest thing from your mind. After receiving an unfavorable doctor report, lying prostrate in worship may not be what you feel like doing, but my admonishment is the reverse. Sincere worship is the best way to penetrate sorrow and dismay.

Romans 12:1 "I beseech you therefore, brethren, by the mercies of God, that ye present your bodies a living sacrifice, holy and acceptable unto God, which is your reasonable service."

The fact of the matter is that real worship is not to make us feel good, real worship is designed to make God feel good. The luxury of worship is this; In God's presence, there is fullness of joy, while blessing the Lord, he happens to give us peace when we are in his presence.

A true lifestyle of worship will cause you to sacrifice forms of media such as television and radio. I am in no means saying that you cannot watch television. What I am saying is that strict moderation is important for a worship lifestyle. More importantly, a lifestyle of worship will sometimes cause you to sacrifice relationships and people that you deem to be very important. It wasn't until I lost some key people in my life that I really experienced the presence of God. It is safe to say that relationships God hasn't ordained, keep us from getting close to him. Suffice it to say that while we may emotionally love and cherish some folk, the Lord will be gradually moving them out of the picture. The wrong people in your life literally prohibit God's blessings because they have become your God. Let me help you understand this concept. For eight years I was in a relationship. I felt emotionally that the relationship was right and from God. Out of nowhere the Lord snatched that person out of my life. On the wake of devastation, I heard the Lord exclaim these words **"NOW I CAN USE YOU!"** God wants to use you, but he will not share you with idol gods.

Psalms 34:18 "The Lord is nigh unto them that are of a broken heart; and saveth such as be of a contrite spirit."

For all of you, who are broken, understand the major theme from the above verse. When you suffer because of a loss, God is very close to you. When situations occur in which people hurt you and walk out of your life, this is the perfect time to position yourself in the posture of worship. The reason why God gets so close to you in times of hurt and pain is because you finally have to depend on him to be your source and that's what God's been wanting all along. Saints of God, hear me good. When God allows something to die, do not try to revive it. As a worshiper, understand that some things were in your life just for a season and now God is ready for another level of worship from you. When the Lord gets ready for another level of worship from you, he will sometimes move in what seems to be a cruel way but just know that it's working for your good. If you are going to walk in the power of worship and be used by God, expect him to move against your wishes. The good thing is this, "once God removes the blockage, he fills the void!" Saints, catch this point. When God fills your void you will never be empty again. People and factors of this world change but God remains constant. In other words, the Lord is the same yesterday, today and forever more.

Exodus 34:14 "For thou shalt worship no other god: for the Lord, whose name is Jealous, is a jealous God."

The above scripture puts it in plain English; God is literally saying, "I am jealous." Now, in order to grasp the point here, we must understand the nature of a jealous individual. One who is jealous will basically do anything to get rid of that which causes him to be jealous. Allow me to illustrate this.

You lose your car, your spouse leaves you, your house is one month away from being repossessed and your job is downsizing. You could very well be experiencing a jealous God. God has a way of removing those things that have become idols in your life. I would like to pose a question here; what is it in **your** life that just might cause God to be jealous? Some of us struggle with relationships, money, our jobs and other things that we are attached to. I deem it necessary to stress that we *should* live in prosperity, but when riches take the place of God, you are on dangerous grounds. As worshippers and believers, we have been "purchased" by God.

*Acts 20:28 'Take heed therefore unto yourselves, and to all the flock, over which the Holy Ghost hath made you overseers, to feed the children of God, **which he hath purchased with his own blood.***"

*1 Corinthians 7:22-23 "For he that is called in the Lord, being a servant, is the Lord's freeman: likewise also he that is called, being free, is **Christ's servant. 23 "Ye are bought with a price; be not ye the servants of men.***"

All three of the above scriptures point out the fact that God literally owns us as worshippers. When you gave your life to Christ you literally joined an army. The rules of most armies do not allow you to quit whenever you get ready! Every time you enter the presence of God, you must have the right attitude towards giving God praise and worship. As a praise and worship leader, there have been many times that I just did not feel like lifting holy hands and exalting the Lord. There have been many factors that have contributed to me not wanting to praise and worship. Some of the common factors that contribute to us not wanting to praise and worship are body ailments, a bad day and pressure from outside sources. The fact of the matter is that we have to constantly keep our flesh under subjection to our spirit. If I allow a headache to prohibit my worship, the headache for the time being, becomes my God. If I have the right attitude to give a sacrifice of praise, I am confident that in the midst of my praise, the Lord will erase the pain. Not only will God erase your pain in worship, like he did for Job, he wants to give you double for your trouble.

As believers, we must understand that God is a jealous God and he will not share his time with anyone or anything. God focuses on our willingness to sacrifice. Worshippers have the attitude that says; *everything I have belongs to the Lord.* For the sake of this chapter, I believe that

Abraham is an excellent example of a worshipper who was willing to sacrifice.

Genesis 17:3" And Abraham fell on his face:"

This scripture validates Abraham as a worshipper as he lays prostrate when receiving the terms of God's promises.

Genesis 22:2 "And he said, Take now thy only son, thine only son Isaac, whom thou lovest, and get thee into the land of Moriah; and offer him there for a burnt offering upon one of the mountains which I will tell the of."

While Abraham had strong relationship with God, he was willing to sacrifice Isaac his son, who was literally a miracle from God. The fact is that Sarah, Abraham's wife, could not have children until God blessed her with Isaac. Abraham's willingness to give up Isaac (who was a miracle) makes the sacrifice even greater. I would like to pose a question here; how many of us are willing to give up our prized possessions? What is it in your life that you would withhold from God? When God says, "let go", do you tighten your grip?

Genesis 22:5 "And Abraham said unto his young men, Abide ye here with the ass; and I and the lad will go yonder and worship, and come again to you."

The first half of this verse is key to understanding the level of relationship that Abraham had with God. My pastor, Bishop Kevin Long, points out the fact that; Even though Abraham was willing to give Isaac up, *he knew that he wouldn't have to* sacrifice his son. The second half of the verse indicates that, both Abraham *and* Isaac were going to return. Abraham and Isaac were basically going to the mountain to have a worship service! Abraham clearly states that he and the lad was going yonder to worship. My point is this; worship gives you an inside track on what God is going to do even before he does it. I submit to you that both Abraham and God *knew* that there was going to be a ram in the bush and the sacrifice of Isaac would not be necessary. I never shall forget. One Sunday morning while in our morning worship, the Lord spoke to me and told me to sow a seed of two thousand dollars.

Both the Lord and I *knew* that the two thousand dollar seed was a sacrifice for me. When I obeyed God and sowed the seed, he assured me that my sacrifice would not even be necessary. I didn't understand what God was saying until three days later when I received an unexpected check for four thousand dollars! As a worshipper, there are some things in your life in which you *must* be willing to give up! Please understand where I am coming from. God already owns what you have any way. He just wants to know that he can trust you with his sacrifice. That fact of the matter is this; once you are willing and ready to give up the sacrifice, the Lord will always provide a ram in the bush. Let me help you understand me. When you meet God's challenge with a challenge, he is challenged to bless you. In other words, my grandmother said it like this; *"you can't beat God's giving no matter how hard you try."* The things you sacrifice to God can never be compared to the blessings he will release into your life.

Saints of God, far gone are the days of the worshipper being broke, busted and disgusted. As worshippers, we should be the examples of God and his power. Part of being examples of the power of God is to literally be a reflection of who God is. Now, it is important for us to understand that worshipping God for material gain is the wrong motive. Although we are not worshipping God for abundant life, we must understand that God works on an "exchange" system. Basically, I am telling you that it is impossible for you to be a true worshipper and not experience the abundant life, or the "*zoe*" which is the ***God kind of life***. In the previous chapter, I pointed out the fact that Abraham was a worshipper. Since we are worshippers like Abraham, there are some things that we are entitled to by understanding God's exchange system.

Genesis 14:19-20 "And he (Melchizedek) blessed him, and said, Blessed be Abram of the most high God, possessor of heaven and earth: 20 And blessed be the most high God, which hath delivered thine enemies into thy hand. And he gave him tithes of all."

Now Abram, whose name is later changes to Abraham, tithes off of the blessing he receives from Melchizedek after winning a great war. Please note that; the first part of the exchange involves our giving of alms. In other words, we as worshippers must realize that the giving of money is one of our highest forms of worship. Worship goes far beyond us lifting holy hands and bowing our knees. Money is essential in showing our appreciation to God. Let me interject a very important point; God does not want just any kind of offering, he wants your best. Notice what happened when people gave God second best.

Malachi 1:7-9 "You have despised my name by offering defiled sacrifices on my altar. Then you ask how have we defiled the sacrifice? You defiled them by saying the altar of the Lord deserves no respect. 8 When you give blind animals as sacrifices, isn't that wrong? And isn't it wrong to offer animals that are crippled and diseased? Try giving gifts like that to your governor, and see how pleased he is! says the Lord Almighty."

In the first chapter of Malachi, the Lord is furious with the way the people have offered unworthy sacrifices. It is important that when you give worship in the form of money, you consider whether or not you could do better. It is funny how we, the children of God, will have well done hair, new clothes and the finest cars but we frown at offering time. In *Malachi 3:8,* we are informed that God has been robbed in tithes and in offerings. Many of our teachers focus on the tithe only and forget about the offerings. I submit to you that if you are a believer/worshipper, not only will the lack of the tithe curse you, but holding back a worthy offering will also curse you. As a worshipper, God is constantly challenging you to give, and in your giving you will receive. If we are going to live in abundant life, it must be understood that praise and worship through giving will prove to God that we will sacrifice. The fact of the matter is that money determines a big part of our emotional and spiritual stability.

*Ecclesiastes 10:19 "A feast is made for laughter, and wine maketh merry: **but money answereth all things."***

I am well aware of the fact that money draws controversy, but until we start using money as a worship tool we are going to constantly be broke, busted and disgusted. Beloved let me tell you; I would not let some metal and paper, which God gave me to start with, hold me back from receiving his presence and blessings. Every seed you plant in worship will manifest itself in tangible evidence.

Worship and Abundant Life

When we, the worshippers, have money, in addition to a few other things, we experience peace, which means; *nothing lacking and nothing missing.* Now, I don't know about you but I can lift holy hands and shout a whole lot better when my bills are paid! It is important to understand that as a worshipper, you are a reflection of God. God does not look in the mirror and see someone who is struggling; he sees a being that is flowing in abundant life. In order to be a true worshipper, you must be a reflection of who God is. It is actually an insult to be a child of God and not flow in the God kind of prosperity. When you are a true worshipper, the manifestation of God's presence will come in the form of prosperity. God does not just want to make you feel good on the inside; he wants your pockets to be indicative of his glory!

When we are willing to give money, like Abraham, we move into the second phase of the exchange. In Genesis the 14th chapter, Abraham tithes. In the 15th chapter, Abraham receives the promise that he will have a son. In the 17th chapter, God gives Abraham even a bigger promise.

*Genesis 17:2-3 "And I will make my covenant between me and thee, and will multiply thee exceedingly." 3 **And Abram fell on his face: and God talked to him, saying."***

Now notice in the above scripture that as God spoke to Abram, he fell on his face and then the Lord talked to him. Beloved, God will speak to get your attention, but when you fall on your face (submit), he will begin to **talk**. Let me clarify. I cordially speak to everyone I pass, but I *talk* to those that will stop and listen. The fact that Abram fell on his face is symbolic of Abram laying prostrate before the Lord, which means that he was in worship as the Lord spoke to him.

Genesis 17:4-5 "As for me, behold, my covenant is with thee, and thou shalt be a father of many nations. 5 Neither shall the name any more be called Abram but thy name shall be Abraham; for a father of many nations."

Now this scripture is very important to us the worshippers and our abundant life. Notice that after Abram falls on his face in worship, he receives details on the covenant and his name is changed. I submit to you that the changing of Abram's name to Abraham is symbolic of him going to another level in the presence of God. In other words, Abram's worship excelled, therefore his quality of life went to another level. I don't believe that Abraham would have been able to get the details he got from God without being on his face. I would like to propose that God himself entered the room with Abraham and because no one can look on God's face and live (*Exodus 33:18*), Abraham *had* to be face down. And like Moses, Abraham received a great level of revelation while he was in the glory of God. We as worshippers must realize that once we have had a real encounter with God, our quality of life must change because we have received another dimension of revelation. The more God reveals about himself, the more power, anointing and abundant life we receive. As God reveals more of his presence, you will become more and more enticed by his glory. Understand that the more you experience the glory of God, the richer you become; not just in feelings but also in the pocket. *Proverbs 10:22 "The blessing of the Lord makes a person rich, and he adds no sorrow with it."* I submit to you that the greatest blessing the Lord can give you is his presence. There is only one way to enter into his presence and that's praise and worship. When I receive God's presence I receive His blessing. As long as I have his blessing, I have got to be rich.

"Abraham is My Daddy"

*Genesis 17:6 "And I will make thee exceedingly fruitful, and I will make nations of thee, and **kings shall come out of thee."***

*Romans 4:16 "Therefore it is of faith, that it might be by grace; to the end the promise might be sure to all the seed; not to that only which is of the law, but to that also which is of the faith of **Abraham; who is the father of us all."***

In understanding God's *"exchange system"* with us the worshippers, we must understand how we are tied to the promise that God made to Abraham. In the above scriptures, Genesis let's us know that kings will come out of Abraham. Abraham, who is a worshipper, can only give birth to individuals who are worshippers. The scripture from Romans references that Abraham is the father of us all. If Abraham is the father of us all and kings were promised to come out of him, it is safe for us to say that we, the worshippers are the kings! When God made Abraham the promise, the promise was forever. The only thing blocking us from our promise is our lack of worship. I don't know about anyone else, but there is no way that I can have a key to a treasure and not open it. Saints understand that, in your worship, you have a key to an inheritance. If we could really see what the Lord has for us, we would forget temporal things and enter into his gates with a new level of thanksgiving. Let me put this in laymen terms. My earthly father owns houses and land. He has made it clear to me that whatever he has also belongs to me. In other words, I have entitlement to my daddy's property. When my father passes, I will automatically be a beneficiary to his assets. My point is that Abraham has passed. The worshippers are his spiritual children. So it's time for us (the worshippers) to walk in our inheritance. *Remember, your daddy was a worshipper, worship is in your blood and you are a "king's kid."*

Hearing God in Worship

Now understand that worship allows you to hear from God and know what he is saying and when he is saying it. In the New Testament, Jesus, while speaking to crowds, would constantly say "he that hath an ear let him hear what the spirit saith to the church." It is quite obvious that everyone in the crowd had physical ears. Jesus was addressing those who could hear in the spirit. Since Jesus is no longer in the flesh, we must be in the spirit in order to hear what he is saying. By being in the spirit, we are in the presence of God. In order to enter the presence of God you must be a worshipper! I am a firm believer that there are some business ideas that only the worshippers can hear. I have to keep reiterating that as a worshipper you are constantly in the presence of God. Being in God's presence is much more then a good feeling; it actually is conducive to profitable revelation. Profitable revelation can be interpreted as *abundant life*! In my free time, I like to sale real estate. A year ago as I was showing a house to one of my clients, I heard the Lord speak to me. He simply said, "this is your house." I had a major problem with what the Lord had said because I already owned a home on the other side of town. It wasn't until I was in the house again that the Lord spoke the same words. I took heed and made an offer on the house. The Lord told me what to offer and where to obtain the money. To my surprise, my offer was accepted and one month later I owned two homes in the same city without a financial struggle! What the Lord is saying to the worshippers is that, he has so much in store for us if we will only get in his presence. God is not looking for you to figure out anything. All God wants you to do is **worship and watch the blessings overtake you!** I don't want to belabor the point of being a blessed worshipper. But understand that whenever God moves, it's always marvelous in our eyes. What the Lord wants to do to you, the worshipper is fascinating; he wants to make an example out of you. Listen to *Hebrews 11:6 "But without faith it is impossible to please him: for he that cometh to God must believe that he is, and that he is a* **rewarder of them that diligently seek him.***"* Saints, it is safe to say that the diligent seekers are the worshippers. Understand this major point. God has many rewards for you. The Lord is excited about blessing you when you bless him. I encourage you to walk in the prosperity allotted for the diligent seekers (the worshippers).

Deliverance, it's In the Praise!

In the wake of this chapter, I need you to understand that there is nothing you can struggle with that the power of God, through praise, can't destroy. It is important to realize that adversity comes to an individual to test his/her level of commitment to praise! The Lord wants to know that when you are encountered by a test, praise will still be your priority.

2 Chronicles 20:1 "It came to pass after this also, that the children of Moab, and the children of

Ammon, and with them other beside the Ammonites, came against Jehoshaphat to battle."

In this scripture, Jehoshaphat, who is the king of Judah (which means praise), has received a word that; he and his people are going to be invaded by a great army. The powerful revelation concerning this invasion is that the invaders are attacking Judah. Now, we must understand that since the word Judah means praise, the implication is that the enemy will always attack your praise! If the enemy can destroy your praise, he can enter your soul and cause you to doubt. Understand that your soul is your *will* and where your affections are concentrated. If your affections are set on doubt, death becomes your fate. When we the praisers doubt, we become prey for the devil. We must realize that when we are under attack by the enemy, it is imperative to go into a season of praise and worship in order to talk to God and hear from God.

2 Chronicles 20:5 "And Jehoshaphat stood in the congregation of Judah and Jerusalem, in the house of the Lord, before the new court."

When I read the above scripture, it blew my mind! Jehoshaphat did something very powerful. When he understood that there was going to be an attack on his praise (Judah), he engulfed himself in praise! Saints of God, did you hear what I just said? When you know there is going to be an attack on your praise, began to praise like never before! If you notice the (a) portion of the 5th verse, Jehoshaphat stood in the congregation of Judah; in other words, he surrounded himself with a praising people! Not only that, he was in the presence of the Lord because he was in the house of the Lord. As worshippers, when we are in praise, we are in the house of the Lord in the spiritual realm. As I stated in previous chapters, when we are in the presence of God, we hear God and God hears us. Since Jehoshaphat had entered into God's presence, notice how he structures his worship.

2 Chronicles 20:6-7 "And said, O Lord God of our fathers, art not thou God in heaven? And rulest not thou over all the kingdoms of the heathen? And in thine hand is there not power and might, so that none is able to withstand thee? 7 Art not thou our God, who didst drive out the inhabitants of this land before thy people Isreal, and gavest it to the seed of Abraham thy friend for ever?

Now I really like Jehoshaphat because he provokes God through a question style of worship. After each verse in the above text, Jehoshaphat leaves a question mark as if he is causing God to think about who He (God) is. Jehoshaphat uses a form of worship that we, the believers, should take special note of. Notice that, while building God's ego, he reminds God of his power and past promises. Jehoshaphat realizes some important factors; one being that Abraham is his daddy! Through this peculiar form of worship, Jehoshaphat informs God of what he promised Abraham years ago. We must realize that when we are faced with a test, it is important to mix praise, worship and God's past record together. I believe that God get's a kick out of his past victories and he is anxious to conquer so much more on our behalf. Because Jehoshaphat worshipped, he moved the hand of God.

2 Chronicles 20:17 "Ye shall not need to fight in this battle: set yourselves, stand ye still, and see the salvation of the Lord with you, O Judah and Jerusalem: fear not, nor be dismayed; tomorrow go out against them: for the Lord will be with you."

Now, this text shows that the Lord promises victory to Jehoshaphat and Judah. We must catch a vital point here; the word of the Lord did not come to Judah until there was worship. Once Jehoshaphat invoked the presence of God, he *and* Judah got a solid word from the Lord.

2 Chronicles 20:18-19 "And Jehoshaphat bowed his head with his face to the ground: and all Judah and the inhabitants of Jerusalem fell before the Lord, worshipping the Lord. 19 And the Levites, of the children of Kohathites, and of the children of the Korhites, stood up to praise the Lord God of Isreal with a loud voice on high."

The 18th verse is crucial to understanding how God works and moves on behalf of the community of praise. The people of God have their faces to the ground. After receiving a victorious word from the Lord in verse 17, Jehoshaphat has another worship session in order to get detail from the Lord. The Lord will speak deep revelations to us but we must continue to worship in order to get the conclusion of the matter. Let me give you a powerful revelation; **"Continual worship is essential to being able to continually hear from God."** When you are able to hear from God, he will show you exactly what to do in order to defeat the enemy.

*2 Chronicles 20:21-22 "And when he had consulted with the people, he appointed singers unto the Lord, and that should **praise the beauty of holiness**, as they went out before the army, and to say, **Praise the Lord; for his mercy endureth for ever. 22 And when they began to sing and to praise**, the Lord set ambushments against the children of Ammon, Moab, and mount Seir, which were come against Judah; and they were smitten.*

The above scripture gives us something to shout about. In verse 21, the Lord gave specific instructions for Judah's deliverance. In verse 22, as Judah was obedient, the Lord showed himself mighty and destroyed their enemies. Notice that Judah didn't use any physical weaponry, they simply praised the Lord and were found victorious. The Lord is not concerned with your clout or your means of economic empowerment. On the spiritual side of things, he is looking for someone who will trust his hand. Before you experience major victory, you must experience major adversity. My point in all of this is for us to grasp the concept that; God has everything under control even when we can't see his methods.

Worship in the Fire

Upon reading this chapter, I need you to understand that worship during adversity is an implication of your true commitment to God. It is obviously easy to worship Christ when everything is going well in your life. In many cases, it does not take a lot of exalting or admonishing in order to get an individual, who has peace, to worship God. The question is; *what happens when you are in the fire of life?* The fire of life can be described as adversity on every hand. How many of us can lift up holy hands and shout when all hell has broken loose in our lives? How easy is it to "shout unto the Lord with a voice of triumph" when you have lost your voice crying the night before? I propose to you that it takes a **real relationship with God** in order to maintain solid worship in rough situations. An example of people who worshiped in the fire is the story of the "Three Hebrew Boys", Shadrach, Meshach, and Abednego. The third chapter in the book of Daniel gives us the story of three men who were in charge of the affairs in the province of Babylon. These three young officers of the city refused to bow down to a golden statue.

Daniel 3:6 "Anyone who refuses to obey will immediately be thrown into a blazing furnace."

In Daniel 3:6, King Nebuchadnezzar had made it clear that everyone in the city must bow to the golden statue or suffer the consequences of being scorched to death. In our lives, there are some golden statues that have a message of, "bow down or else." Your statue may be a spouse who has demanded that you replace God with him/her. Your statue could very well be your job, that says you must work on Sundays or else. The underlying messages from our statues are to give them God's glory. I challenge you now to take inventory and find those things that are striving for God's glory.

*Daniel 3:15 "I will give you one more chance. If you bow down and worship the statue I have made when you hear the sound of the musical instruments, all will be well. But if you don't you will be thrown immediately into the blazing furnace. **What god will be able to rescue you from my power then?"***

Here, the king proposes a challenging question; "What god will be able to rescue you from my power?" Understand saints of God that the devil will speak to you and challenge your worship by challenging your faith. Notice in Daniel 3:15; the letter "g" in the word "god" is lowercase. The devil will always try to minimize your God and his power. The lowercase "g" implies that our heavenly father (the almighty God), is on the same level as the worlds (lowercase "g") god. The fact of the matter is that our God (uppercase "G"), has all power and cannot be minimized, no matter how others try to devalue him. The challenge for us, as believers, is to stand on what we know.

Daniel 3:16-18 "Shadrach, Meshach, and Abednego replied, "O Nebuchadnezzar, we do not need to defend ourselves before you. 17 If we are thrown into the blazing furnace, the God whom we serve is able to save us. He will rescue us from your power, Your Majesty. 18 **But even if he doesn't**, *Your Majesty can be sure that we will never serve your gods or worship the gold statue you have setup."*

As worshippers, the Three Hebrew Boys are rigid in their stance. They let the king know that their God is able to deliver, but even if he doesn't, they will not bow down to the statue. I wonder how many of us have, "even if he doesn't worship?" "Even if he doesn't worship" is true and sincere because we are moved to love God for who he is and not just for his delivering acts. When you demonstrate "even if he doesn't worship", you let God know that your love for him is unconditional. An unconditional love for God is the model of what true worship is. How many of us can truly say that our feelings for God are not predicated on whether or not he takes us out of certain situations? The proposed question is tough because it forces you to look within yourself for the answer.

Daniel 3:20 "Then he ordered some of the strongest men of his army to bind Shadrach, Meshach, and Abednego and throw them into the blazing furnace."

This gives us great insight on how real worship can *get you in trouble*. Not only are the boys thrown in the fire, but also they are tied up. The point is this; when you choose to give your all to Christ, the world and its systems will seek to literally bind you in ropes and chains of structure. A few years ago, they took prayer out of schools. This was an attempt to bind the Christian community. When the devil ties you up, he wants to force you to live in a certain mold. The devil does not appreciate you living a free life. The Lord, on the other hand, desires that you live a bondage free life. That is why *2 Corinthians 3:17* asserts that; *where the spirit of the Lord is there is liberty.* Even in worship services, many people have problems lifting up their hands because the devil has literally tied them up in the spirit. When you allow Satan to bind you, he has the ability to take away your praise thus making you powerless in an evil world. On the other hand, while Shadrach, Mechach and Abednego were bound physically; they still maintained an attitude of worship while going into the fire. You may be on a bed of affliction; you need to know that your attitude of worship and thanksgiving has the power to raise you up! It is the mentality of worship that breaks the chains of bondage in our lives. No matter what the devil tries, you able to say like David, *"I will bless the Lord at all times, and his praises shall continually be in my mouth."* In my spiritual imagination, I'd like to think that while the Hebrew boys were in chains of bondage, there mouths were free to magnify and exalt their heavenly father even while being tossed in the fire. As we go into fire in our lives, we must learn to live Paul's quote *"In everything give thanks for this is the will of God in Christ Jesus concerning you."*

Daniel 3:25 "Look!" Nebuchadnezzer shouted. "I see four men, unbound, walking around in the fire. They aren't even hurt by the flames! And the fourth looks like a divine being!"

The 25th verse gives us the grand finale. Notice that Nebuchadnezzer, the offender and enemy of the three men, saw them bondage free first. God knows how to show you to be blessed right in front of your enemies. Nebuchadnezzer had to acknowledge the fact that he was powerless against the God of the Three Hebrew Boys. God, the fourth divine being, got in the fire with Shadrech, Mechach and Abednego. I would like to pose a question; If God got in the fire with the Three Hebrew Boys, what makes you think that he won't get in the fire with you? When you are a true worshipper, you literally sanction God to get

82

in the fire with you! What I like most about God is that he is a protector of his own. We serve such an awesome God; a God who won't put us in a fire to be consumed. The fact of the matter is that God allows fire in our lives to show his delivering power. If you can, visualize this; God put you in fire to consume the fire. The important thing to keep in mind about fire is this; *fire added to fire is just more fire!* (You may need to read the prior sentence again). When you conquer problems in your life, you are made to be a hotter, larger flame than you were before the problem. Let me tell you something. The more you go through and experience, the more anointed flame you have. After a few hot situations, you literally become a consuming fire in which everything you encounter is burnt to a crisp. What ever you do, *remember to worship in the fire!*

In summary, we have to understand that Shadrach, Mechach and Abednego, did not have any ulterior motives for worshipping God. In other words, the three Hebrew Boys were not looking for a blessing in response to their actions. They asserted that, if God did not deliver them, they knew that he was able and they refused to bow to a gold statute. Although the boys were not searching for a blessing, the ways of God are to reward his diligent seekers.

Daniel 3:30 "Then the king promoted Shadrach, Mechach, and Abednego to even higher positions in the province of Babylon."

Notice that Nebuchadnezzar (the enemy) was literally forced to bless Shadrach, Mechach and Abednego. God has a way of making your enemies your footstool and causing them to be at peace with you. Before going into the fire, the Hebrew Boys held adequate positions in the province of Babylon. After coming out of the fire, they were promoted to higher positions, which meant better lifestyles. After you come out of the fire, the Lord has a great reward for you. Many of us will be like Job; "we are going to get *double for our trouble*." Your unconditional worship releases you into conditional blessings. Allow me to simplify my statement, sincere worship moves the hand of God to bless you abundantly! When you give God everything you have with no strings attached, he is moved to promote you to higher heights and deeper depths. God has so much in store for the sincere worshipper.

Joy in His Presence

It is important that we understand and realize that there is joy in God's presence. *Nehemiah 8:10 "The **Joy** of the Lord is your strength."*
Psalms 16:11 "In thy presence is fullness of joy."
I have italicized the above verses to make a simple but powerful point. We have already established that, when we give God true worship, we establish a rite of passage into his presence. Psalms 16:11 asserts this fact; In God's presence, we experience the fullness of Joy. I now must pose a question. What exactly is the advantage of experiencing the fullness of joy? Nehemiah 8:10 proclaims that the joy of the Lord is your strength! Allow me to make a connection here. When I am

in God's presence, I have joy. If I have joy, I have strength. Strength is essential to getting anything done. When I have strength, I can accomplish the various tasks in my life. The stronger you are, the more you can handle. In plain English, if you have the proper amount of strength, you can move any situation in your life! The overall admonishment here is for every individual to understand the importance of staying in God's presence. When you are in God's presence you are like the athlete that works out constantly. When you consistently exercise in God's presence, you have the strength to run the race that God has set before you. While running the race, it is essential to understand that the stronger you are, the more you can endure while reaching your overall destiny. Saints of God, you can overcome any obstacle in your life by hearing God in worship and responding to him in praise. On the eve of this discussion, I want you to understand that praise and worship is the answer to all of life's difficult questions. With the proper worship, you will become sensitive to the spirit of God. With the proper praise, you will conquer everything that stands in your way. It is my prayer that you excel in the presence of God like never before. At this point, I hope you understand that no matter what you are facing; our God is worthy to be exalted. As you make a paradigm shift, understand that everything is working out for your good. I challenge you as a worshipper to take every revelation in this book and go to new dimensions in God's presence. And remember, **"GOD WANTS TO TAKE YOU HIGHER!"**